This book
belongs to:

Color With Me! Grandma & Me Christmas

Mary Lou Brown
Sandy Mahony

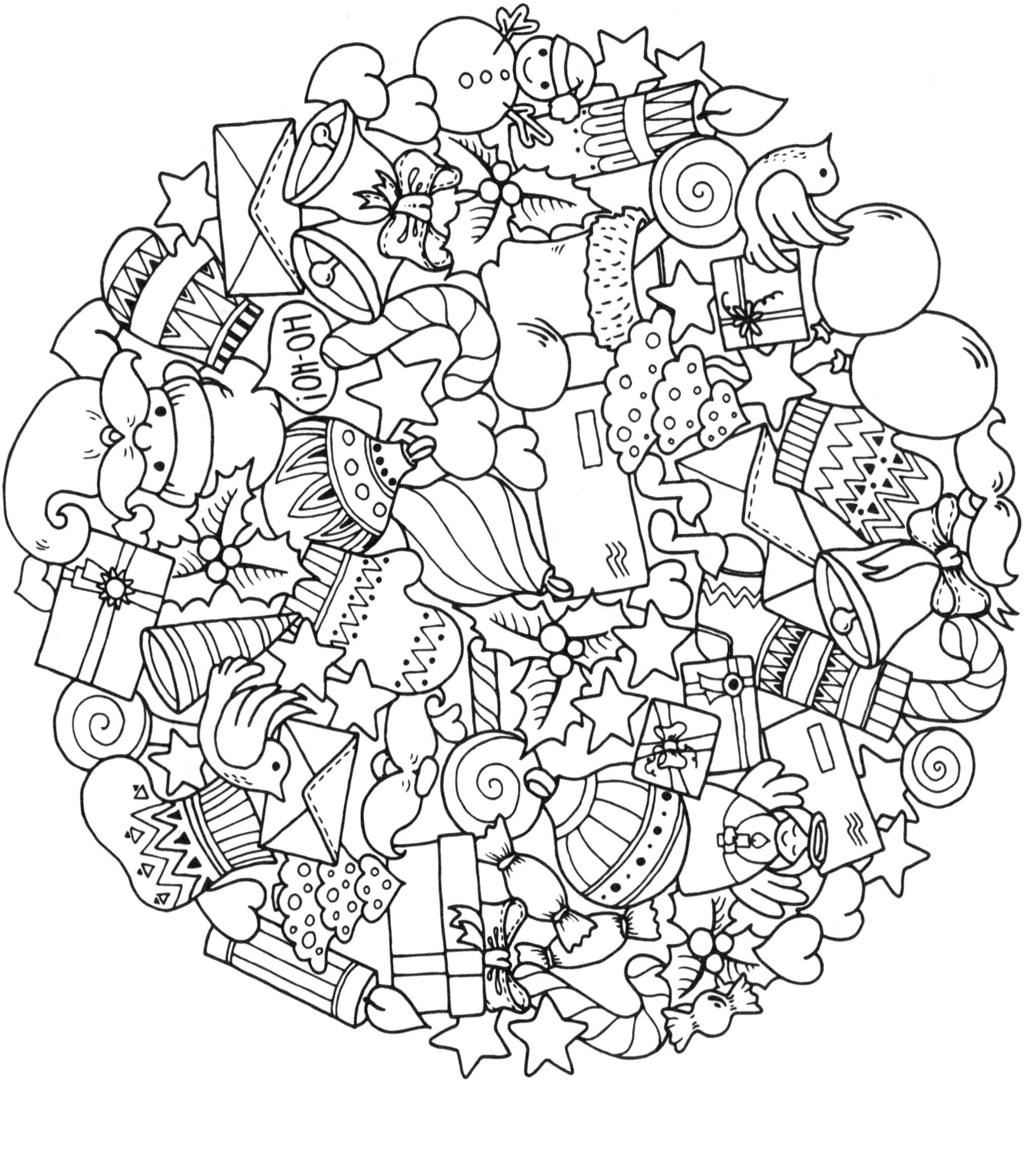
HO-HO!

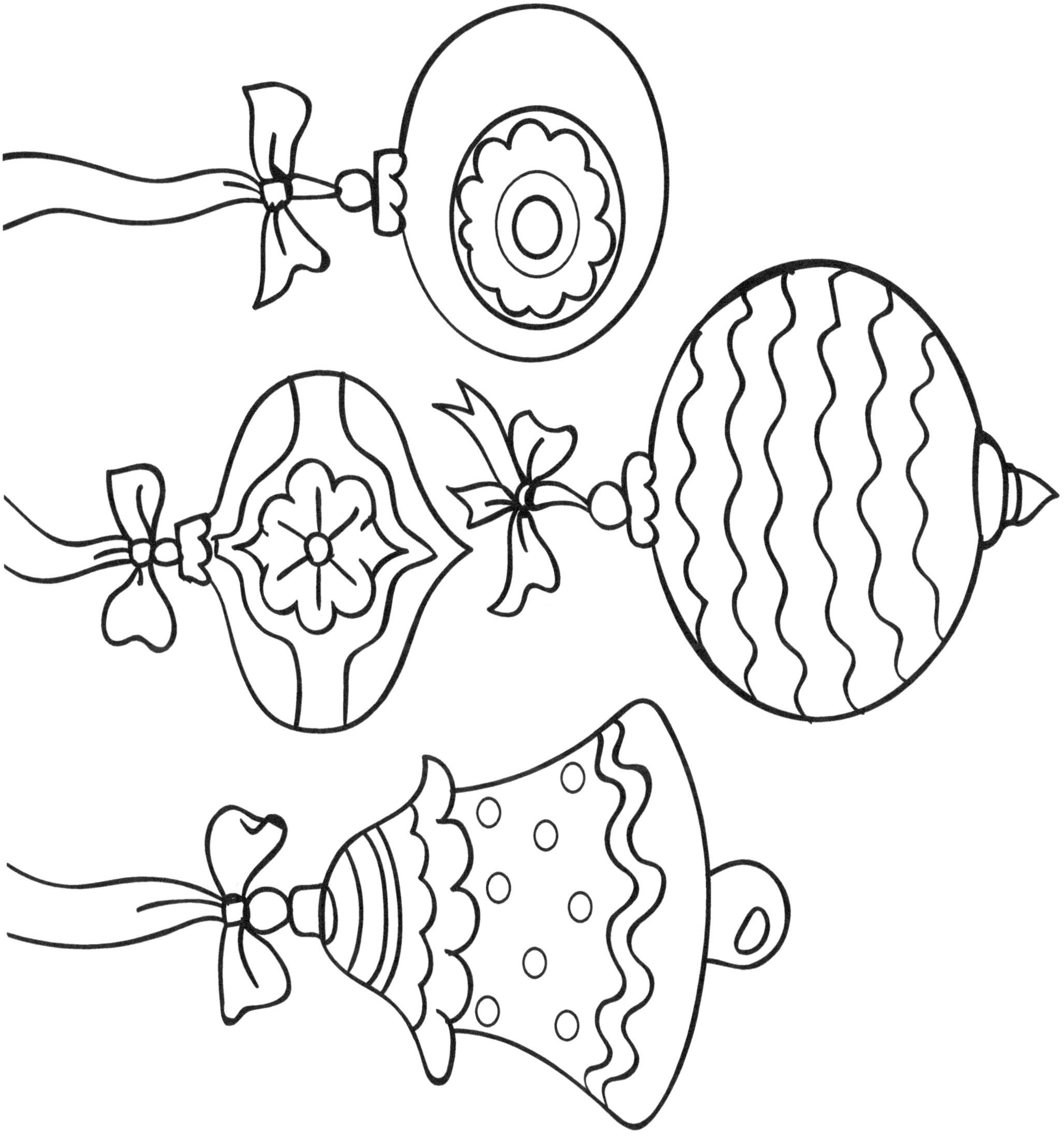

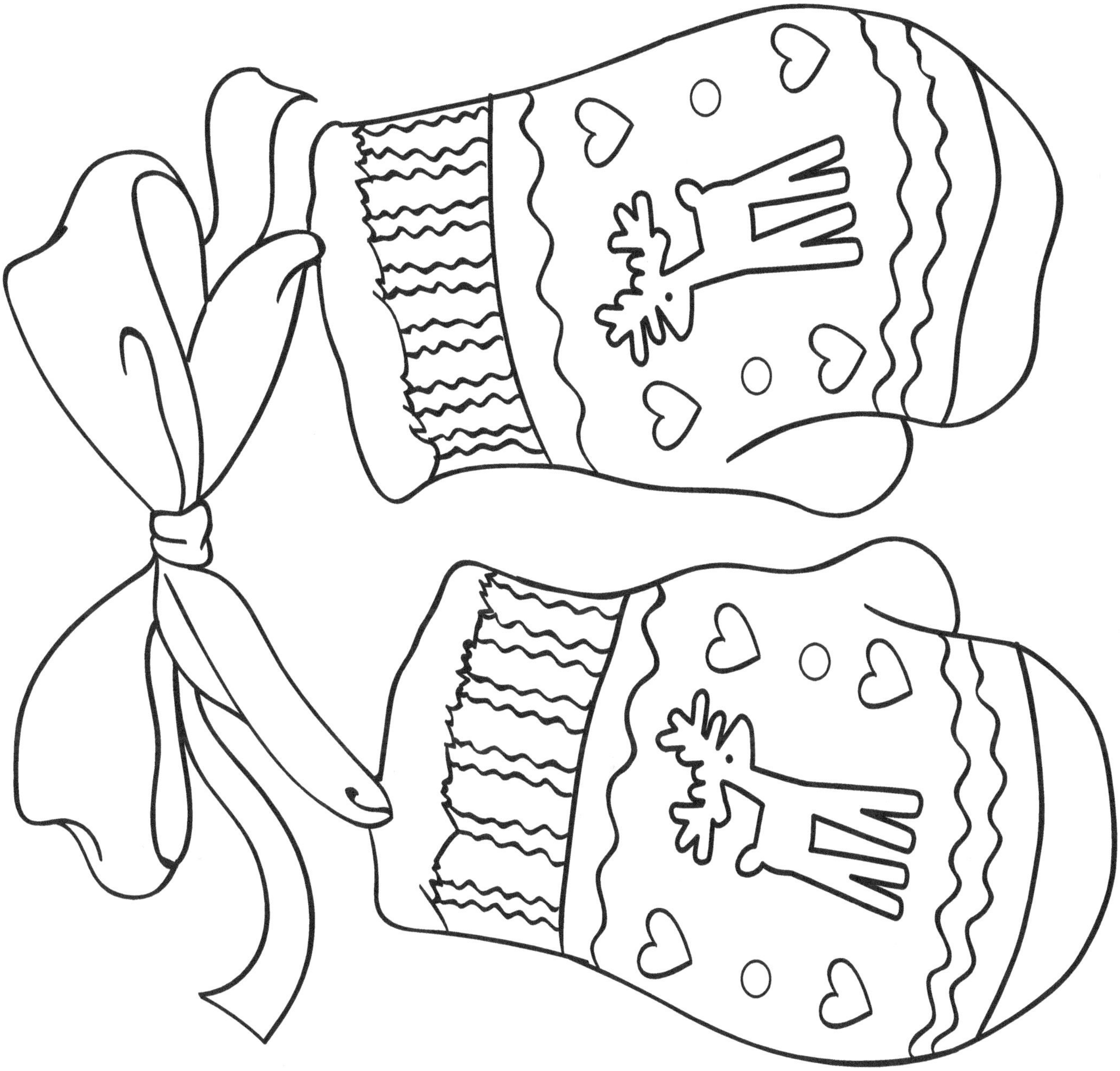

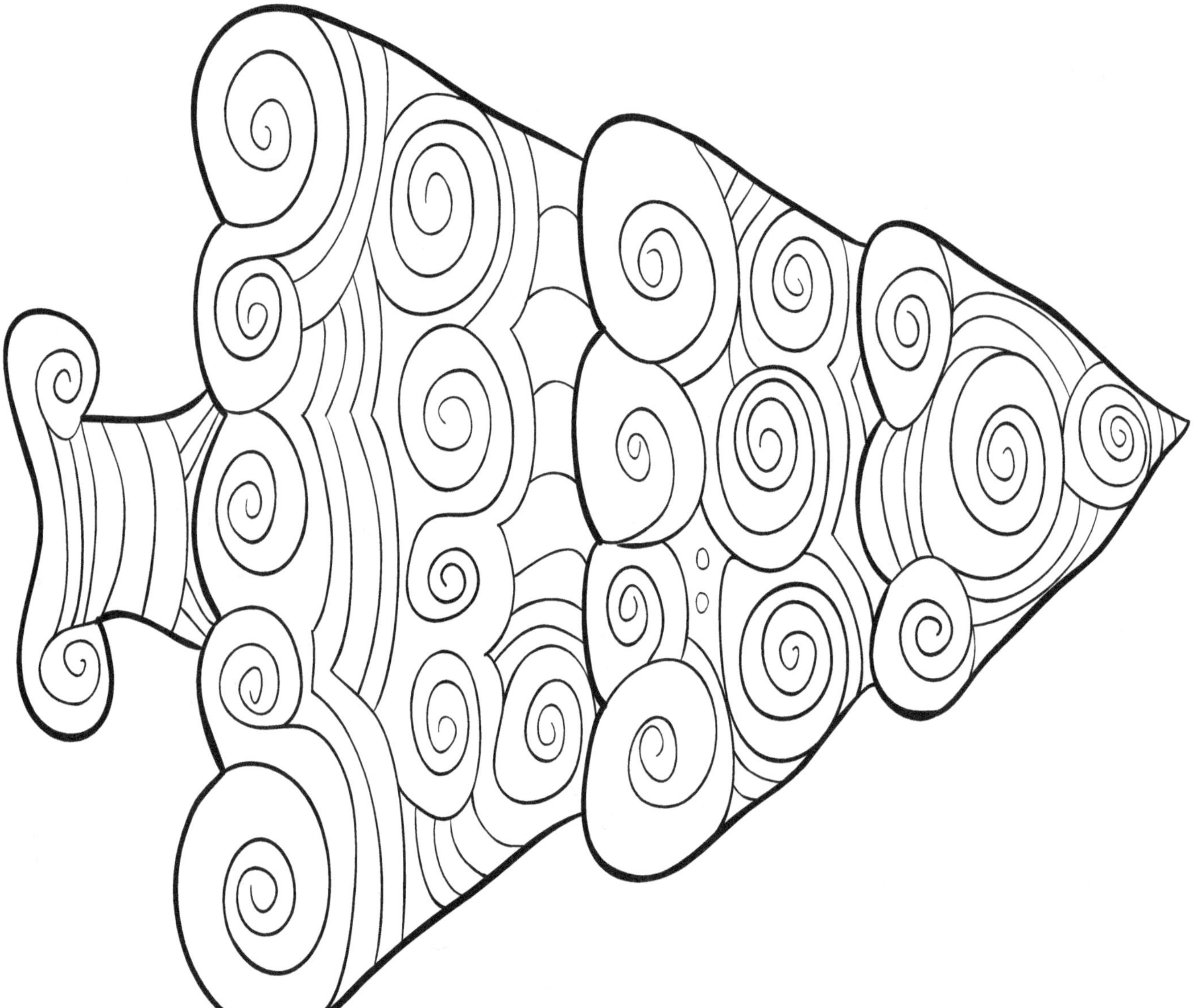

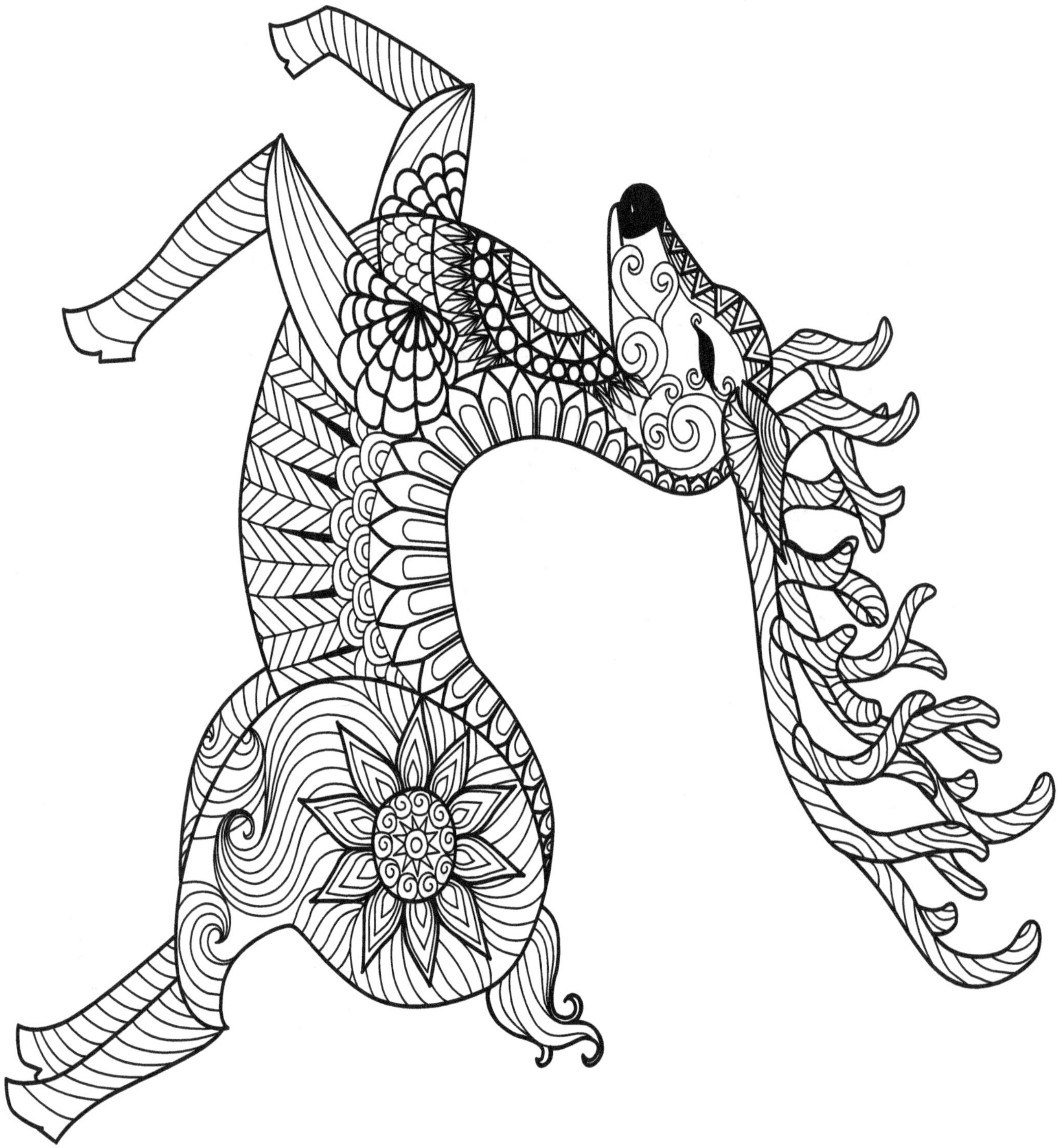

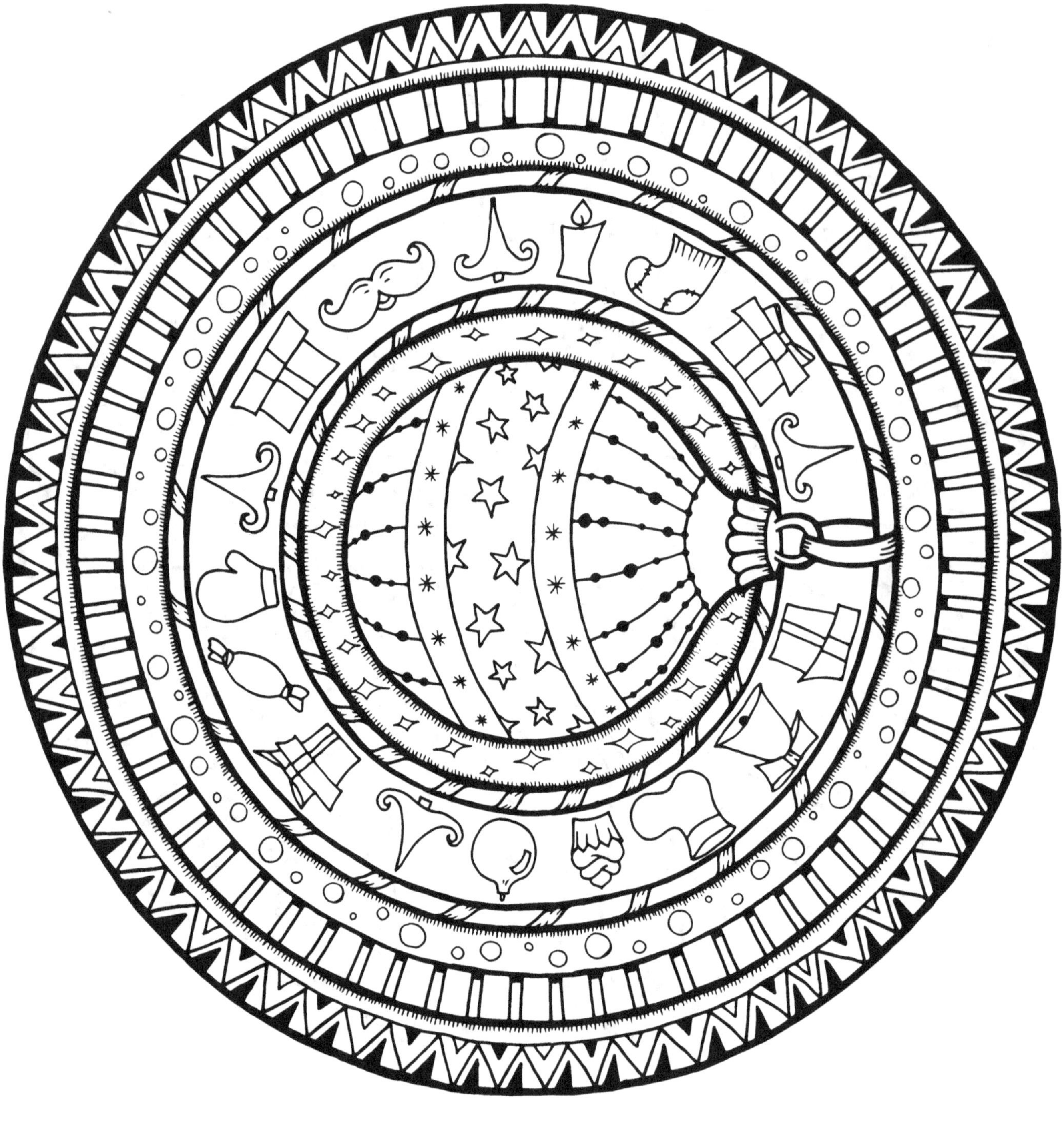

adventurelearningpress.com